Nonprofit Quick Guide™

The Surprisingly Easy Steps to Receiving Robust Community Support

Joanne Oppelt, MHA
Linda Lysakowski, ACFRE

Nonprofit Quick Guide: The Surprisingly Easy Steps to Receiving Robust Community Support

One of the **Nonprofit Quick Guide**™ series

Published by Joanne Oppelt Consulting, LLC

ISBN Print Book: 978-1-951978-19-8

13 12 11 10 9 8 7 6 5 4 3 2 1

JOANNE OPPELT, MHA

Joanne, principal of Joanne Oppelt Consulting, LLC, is a seasoned rainmaker with a distinguished track record of success. During her twenty-five-plus years working in the nonprofit arena, she built or rebuilt successful fundraising departments at every stop, helping her organizations grow capacity and more effectively fulfill their missions.

She has held positions from grant writer to executive director at the nonprofits Community Access Unlimited, Caring Contact: A Listening Community, Family to Family Network of New Jersey, Christian Healthcare Center, March of Dimes Central New Jersey, Prevent Child Abuse New Jersey, and Maternal and Family Health Services. Her extensive background in a variety of work roles and organizations enables her to understand the realities and challenges nonprofit practitioners face–both internally and externally. Her success at every stop positions her to help any nonprofit, whether through her books or consulting practice, turn around its struggling fundraising operations.

Joanne is the author of four books and coauthor of eleven. She has taught at Kean University as an Adjunct Professor in its graduate program. She is also a highly sought-after speaker and presenter.

Joanne holds a master's degree in health administration from Wilkes University, where she graduated with distinction. Her bachelor's degree is in education, with a minor in psychology.

Linda Lysakowski, ACFRE

Linda is one of approximately one hundred professionals worldwide to hold the Advanced Certified Fundraising Executive designation. Linda is the author of ten nonfiction books, a contributing author, co-editor, or coauthor of twenty-three others. She has also written seven books in the spiritual and fiction realms.

Linda has more than thirty years in the development field. She worked for a university and a museum before starting her own consulting firm. In her twenty-five years as a philanthropic consultant, Linda has managed capital campaigns that have raised more than $50 million, helped hundreds of nonprofit organizations achieve their development goals, and trained more than forty thousand development professionals in most of the fifty states of the United States, Canada, Mexico, Egypt, and Bermuda.

She served on the Association of Fundraising Philanthropy (AFP) Foundation for Philanthropy Board and on the Professional Advancement Division for AFP. She is a past president of the Eastern Pennsylvania and Sierra (Nevada) AFP chapters. She received the Outstanding Fundraiser of the Year award from the Eastern Pennsylvania, Las Vegas, and Sierra (Nevada) chapters of AFP, was honored with the Barbara Marion Award for Outstanding Service to AFP, and received the Lifetime Achievement Award from the Las Vegas AFP chapter.

Linda is a graduate of Alvernia University with majors in banking and finance as well as theology/philosophy, and a minor in communications. As a graduate of AFP's Faculty Training Academy, she is a Master Teacher.

Dedication

This book is dedicated to the nonprofit leaders who take the time to ask questions and listen to the public, create strong brands, and form mutually beneficial partnerships that lift up the entire nonprofit community.

Contents

Chapter One

The Community Contract

Nonprofit organizations exist to meet community needs, are governed by community members, and are funded through community contributions. Nonprofit agencies leverage their scarce resources by fostering community relationships. Nonprofits even receive a special tax-exempt status based on their involvement with the community. In the nonprofit world, survival is defined by how much community support they receive, financially and otherwise. Knowing how to procure strong community backing is crucial to your nonprofit's success.

Yet the number-one question we hear is, "How do I get the community to support my organization?" Often the question is related to finding new donors. Many times the question is related to creating organizational awareness and gaining public visibility. Other times, the question refers to finding the paid and unpaid staff needed to carry out operations. Sometimes nonprofits need the community to refer potential clients to them. Yet, again and again, we see nonprofits struggle to be widely known as premiere social entities worthy of tremendous community support.

What is Your Starting Point?

To understand how to build strong community support, you need to know where your starting point is: what the community thinks now. So often, community members think of nonprofits as do-good organizations that are poor and unsophisticated, always asking for money. Where people do the work of saints on a shoestring budget. Where there is never enough money to meet all the needs. It's a sad situation. Bless them, trying to beat the odds.

Well, if those are the prevailing stereotypes, no wonder nonprofits have trouble garnering robust and widespread community support. Who wants to support a losing battle?

Come from a Position of Strength

To realize pervasive, robust community support, you need to position yourself as a winner. You start improving your organization's position by clearly communicating, through all your communication channels—even your internal ones—what your organization is and what it stands for. Moreover, you do it in a way that reflects your agency's personality.

You need to communicate a consistent image throughout your organization to steadfastly project that image to the community. You want control over your messaging so that you may influence the community to give you its generous support.

Define Your Value

You get the community's generous support by giving it. It's an exchange relationship. You give and get something of value. So, you need to define the benefits you bring to your different constituencies. Both in terms of what you do and how you do it, and the results you achieve.

Defining your value is easier said than done because people outside the nonprofit world generally don't speak the same communal language as we do. And the corporate cultures are different, meaning they most likely have a different set of collective values than we do. So we must research who we want to talk to to understand their perspectives. This enables us to use words and deeds that motivate *them*, not necessarily us. Only then will we convey an accurate picture of what we have to offer and invite them to enter into a mutually beneficial relationship.

Keep Your Supporters

Once you have people on board, you need to keep them on board. Engage them. Give them something meaningful to do, whether they be volunteers, staff, donors, or advocates. (Tip: You can even engage your vendors by giving them something meaningful to do.) Keep in mind, though, the "something meaningful" needs to be meaningful to them as well as to you.

Then thank them up the wazoo. Treat them as the most important people in your world. Because guess what? They are! They are the heroes of your cause.

Build on Your Success

And then start building on the personal investment they have given and the goodwill you have built, as well as any other benefits they have received as a result of your partnership. Ask them to invite their networks to experience the same sense of fulfillment they have. Attract other community members and organizations by touting the value of the benefits you deliver. Watch your network grow. Observe, one by one, people and establishments commit to working with you.

Yes, it's a lot of work. Yes, it takes time. No, it won't always go smoothly. But if you stick with it, the results are worth it. You will see your public visibility increase. More community members will be aware of what you do and the importance of your work. People will want to work with you. You will have begun a positive, upward cycle of obtaining more and more community support.

Wrapping It Up

◆ Even though it is vital, most nonprofits struggle to gain adequate community awareness and public visibility.

◆ If you want to know how to best reach your community, start by researching your nonprofit's image.

◆ In both your external and internal communication materials, define what your organization is, what it stands for, and the value it brings in ways that your audiences, not you, will understand.

◆ Be consistent in your messaging across all your communication channels, internal as well as external.

◆ Engage and continually thank your supporters.

◆ Results take time.

Chapter Two

Who Do You Think We Are?

In the last chapter, we outlined what many community members think of nonprofits: do-good organizations who are poor and unsophisticated, fighting an uphill battle, always asking for money. And it's no wonder people who hear our pleas for help think that. How many times have you heard, or maybe you've even presented, appeals from nonprofits along the lines of "we need money, or else we're in jeopardy of not meeting our goals" (maybe even the extreme, "We'll have to close our doors"). What kind of message does that send?

Joanne will never forget the time she was defending her request for funding in front of a funder's resource allocation committee for the first time as executive director. The previous year had been a rough one for the agency. When she presented her arguments for more funding, she outlined all her agency's results in the past year. She thanked the committee for their past support and laid out the plans for the coming year. When she was asked about last year's struggles, she acknowledged them and detailed her upcoming plans to fix the rather serious problems. When she was finished, one committee member said, "I'm glad to hear the agency has done so much. And thank you for being so open with us about your challenges. We all had our doubts about continuing to fund an agency that was going downhill. Last year, the presenter talked about the need for money so the agency could survive."

See how the previous presenter had depicted the agency as needy? And the misgivings that created among the donors? Joanne ended up getting the funding she requested at its full amount. She turned around their thinking by coming from a position of strength as opposed to weakness. And the donors responded to that power. The situation of the nonprofit was still dire. And the committee knew that. But the organization was shown as capable of overcoming its challenges and had a plan to face the future. And that made all the difference.

"Our Cause is So Worthy"

Most people understand the dire need for the services nonprofits offer. Maybe not each individual nonprofit agency, but certainly as a sector. Because nonprofits are mission-oriented, as opposed to profit-focused, people can see the dedication and commitment of the nonprofit workforce. None of that is in question.

What is in question is whether being a worthy cause in need of money is enough. You often hear this in statements like, "Our agency does so much good; I don't understand why more people don't support us." Sometimes the appeal for support is guilt-based, like, "Look at all the good we do; you should support us." Or sometimes you get a vague, "Join us in making the world a better place by helping our clients." Unfortunately, none of these statements really defines the *benefits to the donors* that will be realized by supporting you.

In statements like these, you are only appealing to donors based on a limited set of values, which means your cause will appeal to a limited group. Like we said in **Chapter One**, why settle for a fraction of the donor pie? Appeal to more people by appealing to different groups with values other than just doing good. For example, if they're business professionals, they may want to hear about return on investment. If they are municipal or state leaders, they will want to hear about economic development and impact. If they are legislators, they want to hear about how issues affect voting blocks. If they are individual donors, they want to see your organization's social impact on the community. In each case, you need to appeal to the different types of supporters based on the benefits of what's in it for them, not only that you are doing good. Being a good cause is not enough. Not everyone carries the same passion for your cause that you do. You need another way to reach them. Telling them what's in it for them usually works. We talk more about developing mutually beneficial partnerships in **Chapter Five**.

The Big Bureaucracy

At times, you may hear some variation of, "Nonprofits just don't use resources wisely because they're so bureaucratic. It takes forever for them to make decisions." Where in the world would they get an idea like that? Perhaps from their experiences as board members.

Often, board members are not onboarded correctly and think they must make the day-to-day decisions of the agency. Or the board chair is inexperienced in controlling group discussions. Or there is no agenda for the meetings. Or one topic keeps being revisited even though a decision has already been made. And the result is that board meetings may go on aimlessly for hours. People end up feeling that they are doing nothing meaningful.

Joanne remembers one of her friends, an ex-board member of a nonprofit, tell her about what board meetings were like for her. That they droned on and on. And how the poor executive director couldn't buy office supplies without board approval. If the executive director bought them anyway, he was asked to justify the purchase before the finance committee. The ex-board member felt that she was wasting her time on trivial things, which is why she now bears the title *ex*-board member. And now, here she was telling Joanne about the inadequacies of that particular organization. How much do you want to bet Joanne wasn't the only person she talked to? How much community support do you think she quashed?

Sometimes it's volunteer committee work experiences that lead to dissatisfaction. Decisions may not be made timely, and it seems to take forever to get something done. Staff may not have the authority to direct the needed resources to move ahead. When decisions are always made at the top, a logjam occurs at the levels below. Plus, people learn not to take the initiative if they will be chastised for their efforts. And then they give up. This lack of motivation can happen at any level of the organization—board, staff, or volunteers. Then you have bigger problems. Because if your people are not excited about their efforts, they won't attract other supporters to the cause. In fact, many of them will give up and leave the agency. How many dissatisfied committee volunteers are out there telling stories of their frustrations?

Long story short: onboard your board and committees correctly, make sure board and committee service is meaningful, and give your staff the authority to tap into the resources they need to move ahead.

Lack of Business Savvy

Sometimes we hear, "The only difference between nonprofits and for-profits is their tax status. If nonprofits were run like businesses, they would have more money."

A statement like this assumes nonprofits have little understanding of fundamental business principles, lack an overall business strategy, or are poor business managers. In fact, the difference is that a for-profit's surplus operating income goes into the hands of the business owners, while a nonprofit's surplus operating income must be invested back into the agency's mission.

In most cases, for-profit businesses are perceived to have more resources available for operations than do nonprofits. And that may be true. However, nonprofits are often not given the generous financing agreements for-profits are. For example, for-profit government contracts generally, although not always, include enough available funding to cover overhead expenses. Government contracts available to nonprofits typically do not contain adequate funding to completely cover those same costs. And there are often added compliance costs for nonprofits that are not levied at for-profits—for example, financial audit and reporting requirements. However, that does not mean nonprofits are inept. It means they are given fewer resources to start with while needing to do more with them. No wonder they're perceived as poor do-gooders.

Nonprofits have to overcome this perception of poor do-gooders if we are to attract substantial community support. We cannot come from a position of weakness and expect great results. We must come from a place of strength.

And how do we do that? We get to know our potential supporters and their perspectives. We state our benefits to them in a language they understand and concepts they value. We elevate the nature of the conversations about us. *We* define who we are and break the stereotypes. *We* start to control our identity. Like when Joanne went before that resource allocation committee and talked about her agency's plans to improve its situation. We'll talk more about creating your nonprofit's image in **Chapter Four**.

Many people think of nonprofits as weak. The way we approach potential supporters may contribute to that image. Limiting our descriptions of ourselves as purely do-good agencies affects the amount of support we generate. How we run meetings and make organizational decisions can determine how we are perceived. We may have less access to venture capital and more difficulty selling stocks and raising prices, to name a few. It is time we take control of the conversation and establish the immense community support we need. And we can do it. All we need are the right tools.

Wrapping It Up

◆ Nonprofits inadvertently weaken their arguments for community support when they make appeals based on organizational needs.

◆ A passionate request based only on your worthy cause limits the amount of community support you will receive.

◆ Onboard board and committee members correctly, make sure volunteer work is meaningful, and decentralize decision-making as much as possible.

◆ You can take control of your organization's image and the conversation about it.

Chapter Three

Here's What You Say

What does the community really think of your nonprofit? What do potential supporters think of you? Do they even know you exist? How do you know? Have you asked them? The only way to confirm your perceptions of what the community thinks is to ask them. You may be surprised at what you find.

Defining Your Community

The first thing to do to find out what the community thinks is to define your community. For best results, you want to ask a broad cross-section of community members. You want feedback from your agency's leadership, staff, volunteers, donors, and service recipients. You also want feedback from external sources, like community leaders, government representatives, neighbors, neighboring businesses, and other nonprofits.

And don't forget about feedback from your competitors. We know in nonprofits that many competitive relationships are also collaborative because many funders like to fund programs rather than agencies. However, even if you are mainly collaborative and see yourself that way, you compete with other nonprofits for scarce resources. For example, have you ever considered bidding on a federal grant? Do you realize how competitive they are? Even for-profits might be your competition; a local gym might compete with the YMCA's fitness program, for example.

You want feedback from a broad cross-section of your community because your community is where you find people to govern, staff, supply, and fund your nonprofit. Nonprofits live and die according to how much community support they receive. Therefore, you want to influence the beliefs and behaviors of as many supporters and potential supporters as you can.

Asking for Feedback

The easiest way to ask for feedback is through surveys and focus groups. Generally, the better you know somebody and the closer the relationship to your nonprofit, the longer the survey they will take the time to complete and the more willingly they will participate in focus groups. If you want to get feedback from the general public, you will need the survey to be short, and you may need to offer an incentive to get them to participate, say a gift card in a random drawing. The same for focus groups. You may need an incentive like a small gift card to get the public to participate. Just make sure your incentive is actually something your participants value.

When you do surveys to the general public, make them short—no more than four or five questions—so participants can easily complete the whole survey quickly. Time is of the essence. Don't expect people who have no affiliation to your agency to give you a lot of time.

There are numerous ways to conduct public surveys. You can have a running question of the month on social media. You can have a popup on your website. You can stand in a crowd and pass them out. You can mail them out with a response mechanism included. You can go door-to-door and ask for feedback. You can buy an email list and send the survey out. The method you choose depends on your organizational capacity and your agency's investment in the results.

When you ask the public for a response, don't expect a high response rate. You may get only a 1 percent response back, depending on the method you use and how well you target your audience.

Listening to the Answers

If you ask a fair number of people about what they think of your nonprofit, chances are you're not going to like all the answers. You asked people to be critical of you. They will. They can see your faults.

Don't automatically discount negative feedback. Don't be defensive. Don't make excuses. Don't try to explain it away. Instead, listen, really listen, to what people have to say about you. At least now you know your reputation and image. Before, you didn't know. Now that you know, you can do something to influence it.

Chances are, too, if you've asked enough people, that you are going to get conflicting answers and opinions. People have different values and perspectives. Tally your responses. Then look at the middle of the bell curve and don't worry too much about the outliers. If there is no bell curve and answers are all over the place, you may not have asked enough people or gotten enough answers. Or you may have a fractured image, which is important to know. Fractured images are a problem because it means the messages the respondents are receiving are mixed. You want one core identity in the community, one core message that people can easily understand and stand behind. We talk more about messaging in **Chapter Four**.

Analyzing the Feedback

Once you have good feedback, you need to analyze it and respond to it. You want to look at your results and ask questions like:

- What do people think we are? How do we define ourselves? Are our perceptions in sync with the community?
- What do people say about us? What is good? What is not so good?
- What results do we want to prioritize? What area for improvement do we want to tackle first?
- What positives can we build on? What are our strengths? What benefits does the community see that we offer?
- What did they say that is bad? What is the root of the problem? Can we address the root cause and change the way we do things? If we can't change things, can we turn the negative into a positive?

When you ask for community feedback, you get valuable information that you can then use as a starting point for making change. For example, you may want to increase an already good image. Or you may want to turn around a negative one. You want to know where to start your journey toward your goal. Your end goal is to attract as many supporters to your cause as you can.

Wrapping It Up

- Survey a broad cross-section of your agency's internal and external constituencies to obtain accurate public perceptions regarding your nonprofit's image.
- Listen to feedback to learn where you stand, not to respond to criticism.
- Tally and analyze responses. Prioritize and act on what you want to change.

Chapter Four

Let Me Tell You About Us

So, now you know what the community thinks of your agency. Is it what you thought? Were there any surprises? What are you going to do to respond to the results? What are you going to do to influence and change the conversation about your nonprofit?

Branding

To successfully effect a change in your image, you need to define who you are to the community. You need to tell your community precisely what you do and how you do it. You need to know the values that permeate your organization and its operations. You need to determine the words, phrases, and symbols that best communicate to the world the essence of your nonprofit.

Your agency's logo may be the most familiar symbol of your essence. And you may think that you should develop a logo based on what the decision-makers like and dislike. Not true. In fact, branding is big business in the for-profit world and can cost hundreds of thousands of dollars. And it is based on careful research and objective data.

To create a logo that communicates the essence of an organization, a branding firm will ask a sample of your nonprofit's internal and external constituencies for feedback, just as we suggested you do in **Chapter Three**. They know the questions to ask to get the best responses. And they have knowledge that we don't. For example, they know that color evokes an emotional response. And that the colors that you use are an essential part of how people perceive you. For a quick and dirty look, Google your logo's color meanings and see what emotions are elicited when people see your logo.

Same with fonts and pictures. What fonts you use communicates aspects of your agency's personality. As do the type of pictures and photos you use in your communication materials. Every aspect of your communication materials tells people something about your organization. A branding organization can help you identify all those aspects. The goal is to come with one unified image of your nonprofit that you can use to tell the world about you. So that everyone in the community who comes across you gets the same message. So that you can start taking control of the conversation about who you are.

If you have the connections and can get a branding firm to do some pro bono work on your behalf, great. You may also be able to garner a capacity-building grant that will cover the project expenses. If you can't get something donated or funded, shop around and find a consultant you can afford. The money is worth the investment. The long-term benefits of good branding that lead to more community support far outweigh the short-term financial costs.

Value Propositions

To entice potential supporters to interact with your organization, tell them the benefits of doing so. As we discussed in **Chapter Two**, only a fraction of the community will interact with you out of the goodness of their heart. Plus, as we saw in **Chapter Three**, nonprofits compete with one another and sometimes with for-profits for scarce resources. Community support, particularly financial support, is one of those resources. Make sure that potential supporters know their investment in you is worth it.

First, define the audiences you are trying to reach. Are you looking for volunteers for board leadership? Do you need talented staff? Do you want to increase your donor base? Are you looking for more volunteers to help with program operations? For fundraising? Are you looking for more clients? Do you want to reach your community partners and other nonprofits? Do you want to strengthen relationships with your business community? Or the media? Are you trying to send messages to legislators? Just what groups, specifically, do you want to engage in deeper relationships with? If you are a large enough nonprofit to have fundraising, marketing, and advocacy staff, make sure you coordinate your efforts across all organizational audiences.

Next, determine the interests of each group. For example, potential board candidates may want to do something meaningful or network with like-minded people. Staff may be looking for meaningful work experiences, good pay, benefits, or social experiences. Community partners and other nonprofits may be looking for ways to leverage resources or expand services to clients. Businesses may be looking for ways to promote their products or services or reduce training costs. Media outlets might be looking for human interest stories about their communities. Legislators may be looking for voter approval. Or something else. Do some research if you have to. Just find out what is important to, and valued by, your target audience. Again, coordinate efforts between marketing, fundraising, and government affairs staff.

Then outline the benefits of what you do and how you do it for each group. You want to communicate how your nonprofit's results benefit them in a way that each specific group will understand and value. For example, you may want a legislator to know you can reach one thousand in your community and 70 percent vote. That legislator may want to be a speaker at one of your events or advocate for your agency to receive funding. Or you may want a healthcare insurance company to know that for every one dollar people invest in your services like yours, the healthcare system realizes six dollars in saved costs through reduced emergency room visits. A contribution to you saves money. Facts like these can be used in both marketing and fundraising materials, particularly the case for support.

Yes, you may have to research facts. Yes, it may take a lot of time you don't have. If you don't have a lot of time, see what types of grant research has been done. Sometimes you can extrapolate answers from there. Or start small, with one target group rather than several. Just like the investment in branding, the investment in determining your value to different constituencies will be worth the effort.

Messaging

Once you have your individual value propositions down, look at them in a broader context, that is, what does your organization say about how it benefits the community, what does your community say about how you benefit it, and what do your competitors believe about you? And encapsulate those answers into one sentence. Try it. We warn you, though, it's harder than it sounds. You'll need to put some thought into it. But, again, just like your research and branding efforts, it's worth it. Because what you end up with is a statement of your organization's unique value to the community. In marketing language, it is known as a unique marketing position statement. In fundraising language, it is the basis for your support case. With a unique marketing position statement, you can influence the public perception of your nonprofit and all the good it does. In ways that make you more than a good cause. Which helps you attract a diverse donor base. You start controlling language and perceptions about your organization. And you start standing out from the rest of the pack.

The key to getting your message across is that it is simple and it is repeated. Like everywhere, in every communication vehicle you use. For example, the logo on your letterhead. The wording in your staff members' email signatures. Your website. Your social media posts. In your newsletter articles. In your press releases. During radio and TV interviews. When you make public speeches. In all your fundraising appeals, including grants, annual appeals, major gift materials, and capital campaign materials. In your marketing and promotional materials. Again and again, repeat the same core message and use the same value propositions, fashioned to be directed to the different target audiences.

You want to make sure you drill the message down to the staff and volunteers inside the organization, too. The biggest and least expensive communication channels for getting your message out to the community are your paid and unpaid staff. Employees spend most of their waking hours at work. Volunteers know your agency from personal experience. They talk to their families, friends, neighbors, and colleagues. Who, in turn, speak with their spouses, friends, neighbors, and colleagues. Remember Joanne's ex-board-member friend who had a bad experience at the nonprofit? How many people do you think heard about it? How many people do you think her spouse told? What did that do for the nonprofit's image?

So, make sure your messaging is consistent in your strategic plan, marketing plan, communications plan, and case for support—especially since these documents lay the basis for your external communications. Also, make sure the language you use to describe your nonprofit is included in your staff and volunteer training manuals because, as we have discussed, staff and volunteers are the best, or worst, mouthpieces you've got.

Wrapping It Up

- Learn how to communicate your agency's essence through branding initiatives.
- Define specific audiences you want to reach and clearly state the benefits to each group in a language they understand and concepts that are important to them.
- Begin controlling the conversation about your agency by developing a unique marketing position statement.
- Be consistent in your messaging.

Chapter Five

I Want You!

To meet the community's needs, it takes a village. No one nonprofit can do it alone. We need community support. We need to develop relationships with a wide array of community members. We need to partner with one another to achieve our mutual goals.

A partnership is an agreement to cooperate so that each party benefits. It is an exchange relationship. Each party gives and gets something of value out of the relationship. You give as well as get. And it requires some level of trust.

You are looking for community support. Your value propositions will outline the benefits you have to offer your specific target groups.

And you will build trust partially through your consistent messaging. You will know what you stand for and how to communicate it throughout your internal and external communications and materials. Everything public about you will send one unified message. People and organizations will know what to expect when they interact with you. You will have a strong brand. Awareness of who you are is growing. All you need now is a way for people to enter into a relationship with you.

Types of Community Support

Community support comes in many different forms. Some members of the community may offer financial support, leading to increased revenues. Others may help deliver services, like staff and volunteers. Some community relationships lead to more referrals, helping you meet or exceed your service goals. You may ask for community support to promote your agenda and advocate for you or your cause. Or maybe you want community members, like clients, staff, and the media, to spread the word about you. Sometimes community support comes in collaborations that decrease costs or leverage resources, increasing organizational capacity. Maybe you want your supporters to attract and recruit other supporters. The list can go on. The point is that you will most likely be looking for many different types of community support, entering into many different kinds of partnerships with a large number of separate community groups and their members.

And each of these groups will have its own wants and needs. Your job is to fulfill one or more of those wants or needs. And you're ahead of the game in letting your potential partners know what they can expect to receive from you. Because you've chosen which groups you want to approach, have researched them, asked them about what they value, and have developed your value propositions. You know, and have told them and will tell them again, how your agency benefits them in ways vital to them. You are ready to discuss relationships of mutual benefit. You are armed to begin discussions about what you can do for them and how they can support you.

Approaching Potential Partners

Broadly speaking, community support can come in the form of leadership service, volunteer service, advocacy, staffing, donations, clients, and community collaborations. For a partnership to work most effectively and last the longest, not only does each party give and take, each party has something in common with you. Each partner is striving toward an overarching goal, that is, a goal that supersedes each individual party's goals. Even though the results of the partnership may be different for each party, you approach potential partners based on your similarities.

People and Organizations with Similar Goals

When talking about approaching potential partners, most nonprofit practitioners automatically think of approaching people and organizations with goals similar to their own. Namely, those who share our passion for our mission and our vision of the future. People and organizations motivated by mission include individual donors, foundations, volunteers, and advocates. Sometimes legislators share our vision of the future as evidenced by the laws they craft and the causes they fund.

An often-overlooked group of people who share your goal of financial success is your vendors. Vendors make good community supporters. They can offer you necessary goods and services at good prices. If asked, they may be inclined to donate to you, either products or cash. If asked, they may also advocate for you or your cause. They regularly interact with you. If those interactions are positive, they may refer clients to you. They may also talk about you with their personal and professional connections, increasing your brand awareness.

Industry associations, such as the Child Welfare League of America, American Hospital Association, or state education association, are great places to generate community support. Especially for advocacy around issues that affect large numbers of organizations like yours. They may also offer training for your staff. Or they may provide technical assistance to you regarding your marketing and communications initiatives.

Another group of potential supporters is people who are interested in community economic development, like a municipal alliance or business special improvement district. In addition to offering a crucial service, your nonprofit contributes to the economic health of your community by providing jobs, buying goods and services, and through payroll taxes. And don't forget about the secondary industries that employees contribute to, like housing, banking, healthcare, education, and childcare, to name a few.

People and Organizations with Complementary Goals

In addition to people and organizations with similar goals, consider approaching people and organizations with goals complementary to yours. Complementary goals may include things like your agency providing housing while partnering with the local food bank to provide food. Or, if your nonprofit is an organic farm, partnering with a grocery store. Or, if your organization is a disability agency, partnering with a medical equipment company. Think in terms of goods and services ancillary to yours.

Sometimes, in addition to similar goals, government representatives also promote causes complementary to yours. As a result, they may be a good source of community support. In addition, you may be able to find potential community supporters among those who benefit from government support for services complementary to yours. They may be outstanding advocates for you. Or they may spread the word about you.

People and Organizations with Similar Needs

Potential supporters who have similar needs satisfied through your nonprofit include clients, staff, and volunteers. Clients use your services and want to see them continue. Staff members need paychecks to pay bills. Like vendors, members of your staff are very interested in your continued financial success. As we talked about in **Chapter Four**, staff make great community supporters, spreading the word about you to their connections. Volunteers may have similar needs, too. For example, high school and college students may need community service credits. Or retired workers may need socialization. Or maybe they want to meet and work with people with values similar to theirs.

People and organizations who join buying co-ops or discount membership groups fulfill their similar needs to save money. You may be able to tap into those groups as supporters for sharing ideas on decreasing costs further. Or, maybe you can approach them to develop deeper partnerships.

Organizations with Similar Markets

A great place to look for community support is the business community. The business community, like the economic developers, is interested in maintaining a healthy economy. Businesses also need visibility, which you could provide through your staff, volunteer, donor, or advocacy base. You may also be able to help them connect with people in your network they want to meet, like wealthy individuals, industry regulators, or legislators. They may financially support you. And they may turn out to be surprisingly strong advocates, depending on the issue. For more detailed information on developing business partnerships, see our book ***Nonprofit Quick Guide: Best-Kept Secrets for Engaging and Retaining Business Donors***.

Together, everyone achieves more. We meet our goals by partnering with others. Potential partners are best approached by building on similar goals, complementary goals, similar needs, or similar markets. Each of these groups will have its own wants and needs. If you know what benefits you can offer that are important to them and have confirmed your perceptions, you are well on your way to asking your partners for robust community support.

Wrapping It Up

- ◆ Strong community partnerships result in strong community support.
- ◆ A successful partnership happens when both parties give and receive something of value.
- ◆ Successful partnerships can obtain needed organizational leaders, volunteers, advocates, employees, funding, visibility, clients, and community collaborations.
- ◆ You connect with potential supporters based on overarching goals.

Chapter Six

Let's Meet

So, you've clearly defined your nonprofit's identity. Your internal and external materials communicate a unified message. You've identified what groups and organizations you want to partner with. Now it's time to approach them.

Do Your Research

To make the most of your visit and make a really good impression, research who you will be approaching before you approach them. Know something about them. You want to know your potential partners' priorities, speak their language, and communicate relevant information about your agency in ways they understand. In addition, you want to show them that you have put some effort into the developing relationship and that the relationship is important to you. Important enough for you to be selective. You will also save them valuable time if you come in with the background facts.

Foundations

Before you approach a foundation, go through their 990s (tax returns) and match your organization's mission and needs to their requirements. Since it is public information, foundations expect grant-seekers to read their 990s and be familiar with them. If you want to get donations from foundations, start with knowing the foundation's mission, interest areas, geographical giving area, and funding range. You can glean all that information from the foundation's IRS Form 990, which can be attained by searching a foundation's website, asking the foundation for it, or visiting a library with a collection of foundation tax returns.

Of course, that's a lot of information to get through. So it may be worth your while to subscribe to a foundation database that can search 990s by relevant categories, like issue, geographical scope, funding range, and others. Two foundation databases that we have found helpful are the Foundation Directory Online and Foundation Search.

Businesses

For-profits are keenly interested in your agency's financial performance. You need to intimately know your agency's financial performance to get the most from the corporate giving relationship. Being able to speak to your agency's financial health puts you head and shoulders above the rest. You need to be able to talk about assets and liabilities, return on investment, profit margin, debt ratio, and growth trends, financially as well as programmatically. If you don't know how to read and interpret your agency's financials, find out how. Read a book. Find a webinar. Go to a training. Anything that will help you to talk in terms of financial performance will pay off.

Another area of performance business partners are keenly interested in is agency market performance. This is where having the community feedback we talked about in **Chapter Three** comes in handy. Business professionals will want to know what your reputation, or brand value, is in the community. They will also be interested in what markets, other than clients, you serve. Think staff, donors, advocates, and collaborators in addition to clients. What services and benefits do you provide to each of those markets? What is your market position in each group? What is your reach? How do you know? What evidence do you have? Who are your competitors? How do you differentiate from them? What makes you unique? We talked about developing unique marketing position statements in **Chapter Four**.

The good news is that if you're doing research on, and getting feedback from, your supporters, you're halfway there. Human resources may conduct employee surveys and have other employees as group information. Your executive director or chief operations manager may have information on agency collaborative partnerships. Or you may already have it for grant narratives. You can save time by leveraging what you're already doing.

Government

How do addressing your agency's issues affect the community and the way it votes? These are the things legislators will be interested in. What issues are important to your community's voters? Who are your agency's constituencies—not only the clients but also other supporters, like advocates, donors, and other partner groups? How big a group is it? How influential is it? What is your reach with group members? What is your influence with them? How are your agency's issues important to the public? The community feedback we talked about in **Chapter Three** can really pay off.

You, as a nonprofit, may not be able to lobby for specific candidates or legislation, but you can advocate for your cause and educate your legislators about community issues. And you can educate your community about legislative issues. Do you know what issues are coming up for a vote? Do you have communication channels already in place that can educate your legislators and other agency constituencies about community issues? You can also write letters to the editor or speak as an expert on issues your organization deals with.

If you plan on applying for government funding, you need to know the regulations surrounding the financial and operational requirements of the funding. The government has particular financial and programmatic restrictions that must be followed. And your agency will, sooner or later, be audited. If you don't pass the audit, you may have to return money that was already spent that you no longer have. Or you may be sanctioned and subject to harsher reporting requirements. Not to mention the PR nightmares that can ensue.

But knowing all the rules and regulations associated with any particular governmental funding allocation is easier said than done. First of all, you need to know the legislation that determined the funding. And you need to know the legislation that the law was built on. And the one before that. Sometimes, you need to go back to legislation that is decades old. It takes a lot of time and effort.

Proofread Your Materials

If you approach potential community supporters with an email or letter or leave printed material with them, check for misspellings and grammatical errors. If you are mailing something, make sure the names, mailing addresses, and salutations are correct. If the basic contact information is not correct and doesn't mean enough to you to know the most basic facts about them, why should they get to know you and your organization? This is especially important when asking for donations. Be especially careful when submitting budgets or other financial information. Do your numbers add up? Is your math correct? Check and double-check. If there are mistakes, the donor might ask, "Will my money be used for what it's intended? How do I know the information is trustworthy if there are errors?"

The most common mistakes are the sloppy ones, like errors in name, address, salutation, spelling, grammar, and math. If you are presenting anything numerical, make sure your math is right. There is nothing more frustrating than having someone get all excited about working with you but be confused about what you want, particularly if it's a donation. Proofread your materials. Then proofread them again. Make sure your communication process includes proofreading and editing.

Have a Good Attitude

It almost goes without saying that when you interact with potential supporters, always be courteous and respectful. People generally respond to other people in the same way they are approached and responded to. Reach out to others when you are in a good mood and you realize what an honor is to have someone take the time to interact with you. People will generally respond in kind. They may even tell you how honored they are that you reached out to them—that you think so highly of them that you believe they can help you in impacting such as important cause.

Exhibit Trustworthiness

You also want to send the message "I can be trusted." According to the Blackbaud Institute, 64 percent of individual supporters research an organization through its website. This means that your website needs to be up to date. And transparent. For example, it is best practice to make your financial statements, audit, and 990 available on your website.

Your brand is your promise to the community. Your brand says, "This is who we are." Remember that every piece of information about your nonprofit should communicate your identity. Ensure you stand out in your partners' minds by using your unique marketing position statement to highlight your agency and its work. If you live up to your brand's promise, you will maintain a good reputation in the community—your brand will increase. And as your brand increases, so will the community's awareness of you.

In your interactions with supporters, be authentic, honest, and forthright. Your integrity is your biggest asset. Do what you say you're going to do. Communicate progress, including delays and failures. Address changes in circumstance, either theirs or yours. Communicate regularly and often. With consistent messaging. And with a reference to the benefits they are receiving from the partnership in language and concepts that are important to them and they will easily comprehend.

Be Direct

When you make your support request, whether it be for a donation, volunteer service, referrals, advocacy, employment, or promotion of your cause, be succinct and direct. You want to be clear and concise so there is no doubt about what you are asking them to do. Most of us say too much. The focus should not be on us. It should be about *them* and *their* needs.

And then be quiet and wait for them to respond. Even if it seems like it's taking forever, let them think and be the first to respond.

They will either say yes, no, or maybe.

If they say *yes,* congratulations. You now have a measure of community support you didn't have before. Go on to talk about the terms and benefits of the partnership and get ready to nurture the relationship. Your goal is to have them involved with you long past the current interaction. You must fulfill your side of the bargain so they realize the benefits you have promised. You want them to feel satisfied with their efforts on your behalf. Over time, you want to be able to deepen the relationship, both getting and giving more. We talk more about what they need from you in **Chapter Seven**. We cover how to deepen the relationship in **Chapter Eight**.

If they say *no,* thank them for their feedback and start asking what their obstacles are. Problem-solve with them on how you might be able to help them remove their obstacles. *DO NOT* try to change their minds. You don't want to come across as argumentative or pushy. Just see if there is anything you can do to help to help them say yes.

If you can't remove the obstacles, ask if there is another way to support you that would be of interest. Brainstorm with them. Especially if they want to help. Our experience is that when you've gotten to this point, they want to help. You have approached them based on whatever your similarity may be. They know what you stand for and what the benefits of partnering with you are. And you are coming across as humble with an attitude of graciousness, helpfulness, and respect.

If the obstacles cannot be overcome, thank them again for the feedback and ask if they would still like you to communicate with them in any way. If they say yes, discuss what type of information they would like, and how often. And then tell them when you will check in again. Then do it. Perhaps the "no" they are giving just means not now. If it does mean not ever, thank them for their time and feedback, tell them you hope your paths cross in the future, and leave. Always leave on a gracious note because you never know what will happen in the future and if you will ever interact with them again. So leave that option open, just in case.

If they say *maybe,* ask open-ended questions. Have you provided them with enough information? Do they foresee obstacles they will have to overcome to move forward? Are the benefits to them enough? Is there anything else they are looking for? Or is the timing off? Are the processes outlined to fulfill the terms of the partnership acceptable? Is the timeline off? Or have you asked them to do something their system can't accommodate? Keep asking questions and providing answers until they have all the data they need to decide, time enough to make decisions given their priorities, and they've figured out the processes they want to be used in both giving and receiving from you.

Before you approach the people and organizations you have targeted for partnership, do your research. Come armed with the knowledge that will be important to them. Always present a polished, professional image. Go in with a good attitude. In conversation, people tend to respond to you in the same manner as they are approached. Be direct and concise in making your request. Wait for them to respond. Then follow up appropriately.

Wrapping It Up

◆ Read a foundation's 990 before approaching them.

◆ When engaging with a business, present your nonprofit's financial and market performance data.

◆ Be aware of issues important to your community's voters when asking legislators for support.

◆ Always incorporate a process for proofreading and editing your materials.

◆ Make your website transparent.

◆ Exhibit authenticity in all that you do.

◆ Make your request clear and succinct.

Chapter Seven

What Do You Want from Me?

Now that you've approached the groups and organizations you targeted and entered into a relationship with them, what do they expect from you? What needs do they have that you can meet to solidify and build your partnership?

Individuals

People are driven by values, feelings, and beliefs. They want to be acknowledged and validated. And they want to be part of something bigger than themselves. Through involvement with your nonprofit, supporters also want assurance that they will be doing the right thing, that their efforts matter, that they will make a difference. Meet them where they are. Answer the questions "How will I contribute to the community good by supporting you? What part of being successful can I share? What will I get that is important to me if I give to you?" As a nonprofit professional, if you can do that for them, they are more likely to be satisfied with your relationship and more likely to keep supporting you. Maybe even getting more involved. People tend to continue to invest in highly satisfying relationships.

Foundations

Foundations are legally bound to the missions for which they exist. If they do not adhere to their legally stated purpose, they are at risk of losing their IRS status. The IRS also requires foundations to give out a certain amount of their corpus every year. That's why the IRS requires foundations to make their tax returns, called 990s, available to the public. So the public knows what they give money to and how they give it out.

It's important to remember that grants are legal contracts. Your organization is bound to perform by the terms described in the grant.

Remember that foundations have legal obligations. And you're the vehicle for fulfilling those obligations. That's why it's so important to communicate changes as soon as possible to funders. It's not because they like being sticklers. It's because they are held legally liable for their decisions.

Businesses

Businesses are interested in making a profit. Corporations are accountable to stockholders who demand they make money. Never forget businesses partner with others because they believe that relationship will result in higher profits. Even though they may have charitable motivations, and many do, resources are scarce to them, too. They need to allocate resources just as wisely as you to do meet their goals. We talked about presenting your agency as more than a worthy cause in **Chapter Two**. For more details regarding presenting your nonprofit to businesses, see our *Nonprofit Quick Guide: Best-Kept Secrets to Engaging and Retaining Business Donors*.

Government Representatives

Let's focus briefly on government representatives.

Legislators

Legislators are in office because of one thing: people's votes put them there. And that is elected officials' primary objective: getting enough votes to stay in office. If you want to get an elected official's attention, talk about what's in the voters' minds. What's important to the community. We covered getting community feedback in **Chapter Three**.

Elected officials also need exposure. Do you offer any fundraising or networking events where they can speak to potential voters? What about your communication channels with clients, staff, volunteers, donors, and partner agencies—can you leverage them?

Government Staff

The other needs and wants you must be aware of to be successful working with government representatives are those of the employed staff. If you go after government funding, the mission of your government-funded program is assumed to be the mission described in the legislation authorizing it. It is presumed that the legislation and the regulations surrounding it are approved by a majority of the voters through their opportunities for public comment. It is the job of the government employees to enforce the will of the people as stated in the legislation and regulations. Government employees aren't in the game to get votes. They're in the game to carry out the government funding according to the rules and regulations. It's up to the government staffers to implement the program as mandated by law.

Government employees are accountable to elected officials and are part of a vast bureaucracy where they probably don't have much control. If you want to get along with a government employee, know all the rules and regulations and follow them. It will make the government employee's life easier.

To solidify a fledging partnership, meet your supporters' needs. Individuals are driven by their values, feelings, and beliefs. Foundations have legal responsibilities to fulfill. Businesses operate to make profits. Elected officials need votes. Government employees ensure compliance with the law.

Wrapping It Up

- If you want people to be satisfied in their relationship with you, acknowledge their values, beliefs, and worth.
- Help foundations fulfill their legal obligations.
- Offer businesses partnerships that will help them meet their financial goals.
- Use community feedback to confirm voting block concerns.
- Research and study authorizing legislation as well as the rules and regulations surrounding it.

Chapter Eight

Keeping It Going

So, you've increased the number of people and organizations supporting you, either financially, by volunteering, through leadership service, by referring clients to you, advocating for your cause, or promoting your agenda. You've worked hard to achieve as much support as you have. You have people on board that you want to stay on board. And attract new supporters.

Say Thank You

The first thing you need to do is thank every supporter for every act of support they make within forty-eight hours of receiving their support. Most nonprofits don't do this. Make sure that your's does. It is common courtesy to thank people when they have gone out of their way for you. They need to be acknowledged and appreciated for that. The number-one thing you can do to ensure that supporters will continue to support your organization is to thank them.

And thank them a lot. Market research shows that it takes seven to ten times for a message to be remembered. That doesn't mean send seven to ten thank-you notes. That means to say thank you through a variety of channels over time. Hold an appreciation event. Send handwritten client notes. Have the board make phone calls. Thank them in your agency newsletters. Thank them at public events. Thank them individually and as a group each time you have the opportunity. Thank community supporters whenever you can. You want them to know how much you appreciate them. Thank and thank again. No one has ever been offended by being authentically thanked too much.

Use the word "you" liberally. Highlight impact. Focus on the needs they met. If you want your community supporters to act on your behalf again, give them what they want. Show them how they are the heroes in making the difference they desired.

Keep the Conversation Going

The key to retaining your supporters is to keep them engaged. People who are engaged are much more likely to repeat, and even increase, their involvement with you. So, how do you engage people in your cause?

Get to know your supporters. Make your interactions personal. Make it a two-way relationship. Ask questions. Answer questions. Tell them the results of what they did and how their time, talent, or treasure made a difference. Give them feedback, so they know their collective impact. Ask for feedback on how the experiences went. Ask them what is meaningful to them and act on their responses. Let them know how meaningful that relationship is to you. Talk to your supporters through text, email, social media posts, newsletter articles, public speeches, and press releases. Communicate, communicate, communicate. Engage your supporters in continuous conversation.

Follow Up with Action

Then go beyond conversation. Listen to your supporters and respond to them by structuring meaningful experiences for them. Find out the motivation behind their actions and structure experiences involving them that meet whatever drives them to respond to you. Don't assume you know what they want. Their wants and needs may change over time. Ask them, again and again, to give feedback, always thanking them for it. Listen to your supporters and respond to them beyond a simple conversation.

Once you start a two-way relationship, continue it. Ask them to do something else to support you, like sharing a social media post, attending a community event, signing a petition, asking a neighbor to join them at an event, or making a donation. Take the relationship to the next level. Then thank, thank, thank, and thank again. Start the engagement process all over again. Thank them, no matter what their contribution. Show them how they made a difference. Ask for feedback. Respond to their motivations. Structure a meaningful experience. Deepen the relationship. Make the relationship stronger. Strong relationships with community supporters not only lead to repeated support, they often mean more support. Think about how that will improve your standing in the community.

Plan for Change

Of course, the only constant is change. If you are building for the long-term, your supporters' needs will change over time. To get ahead of those changes, have your eyes and ears peeled to the community. Constantly scan the societal environment. Regularly get feedback from the community as well as from your supporters. We talked about getting community feedback in **Chapter Three**.

And plan for the future. Take the feedback and plan for going in new directions, exploring contingencies if those plans fall through. Engage in strategic planning. And regularly update your plan. Studies have shown that nonprofits with written, updated strategic plans realize better financial and program outcomes.

So, continually thank your supporters. Engage them in conversation. Create meaningful experiences for them based on their feedback. Deepen the relationship by asking them to broaden their commitment. And plan for changes over time.

Wrapping It Up

- The first step to realizing ongoing community support is to thank your supporters for their actions on your behalf.
- Engage supporters in continuous conversation, thanking them and asking for feedback at every step.
- Provide meaningful experiences for your supporters.
- Engage in strategic planning.

Chapter Nine

Bringing It All Together

To bring it all together, we have outlined the surprisingly easy steps to receiving robust community support. Follow them. And watch support for you and your cause grow.

Step One: Understand Your Image

There are many stereotypical understandings of who and what nonprofits are. The first step in researching your image is to define your community. Then ask that community for feedback. Listen to what they say, even if it is negative. Analyze your findings and take action to fix problems.

Step Two: Define Your Identity

Your brand is your reputation and image in the community. Creating a strong brand will help attract community support. Through thorough branding, potential supporters will have an idea of who you are. Communicating your value propositions to different groups tells potential partners how being in a relationship with you will benefit them. Your best results come from unified messaging. Develop a compelling case for support.

Step Three: Create Supportive Partnerships

Community support comes in different forms, including financial support, employees, volunteers, referrals, promotion of your agenda, advocacy, visibility, collaborations, and recruitment of other supporters, to name a few. You will approach different types of people and organizations to provide different kinds of support. Meet them where they are and approach them with overarching goals. Connect with them based on similar goals, complementary goals, similar needs, or similar markets.

Step Four: Establish Credibility

To meet them where they are, do your research. Foundations, businesses, legislators, and government employees have different priorities. Be familiar with them. Always proofread your materials. Go in with a good attitude. Be humble, exhibit trustworthiness, and be forthright. When you ask for support, be clear, direct, and concise.

Step Five: Address Their Needs

Know the needs of the individuals, foundations, businesses, legislators, and government employees that support you. Design a partnership that helps them meet their needs.

Step Six: Keep Them Invigorated

Thank your supporters for all they do for you. And thank them often. Engage them in conversation and create meaningful experiences they can share in. Continuously follow up with them, thanking them at every step. Constantly scan the community for changes. Have a plan in place to address those changes.

Step Seven: Build on Your Success

When you start out, start out small. Crawl, walk, and then run. Start by targeting one or two potential supporters, entering into a partnership, engaging them, and letting the effort snowball. Start the positive, upward cycle of generating goodwill by meeting your partners' needs and making them the hero of your results. And watch your community support grow.